CW00471590

Building a New Ministry:
And Raising New Leaders.

A Practical & Devotional Workbook

Yinka Oyekan

ISBN: 9781798958407

Bible Copyright

Bible scripture quotations used in this work are from the following. Bibles:

Contents

To all the wonderful people I have had the joy and privilege of pioneering with, you know who you are.

Part 1
BUILDING A NEW MINISTRY

How to *use each section of part one*

1. Each session is meant to last one hour.

2. Each session is meant to be primarily an interactive discussion.

3. Each session is designed to take the pioneer on a practical journey of consideration, inviting them to think through how pioneering could affect them. Open thinking is encouraged.

4. At the start of each session is an explanation of the aims and goals of the session.

FINDING THE TEAM

AIMS OF THIS SESSION: IN THIS SESSION WE WILL DISCUSS THE FIRST STEPS REQUIRED TO BUILD A GOOD, STRONG, UNITED AND FUNCTIONING TEAM.

[A] BUILD A GREAT TEAM

1. **The** first step.

   - **You need to build a team.**

     ₪ Find your team of 4-12 from the community you are committed to.

     ₪ If pioneering a new group, dependant on the type or aim, anything up to 10 adults or 8 families connected with the Ministry / Group could be recruited.

     ₪ Some of the individuals who will help you may be found on the spiritual mission field you wish to engage. They may be broken or wounded, but with some support and help they could return to the front line.

2. **The** second step.

   - **Facilitate relationship building.**

     ₪ Build great social foundations into the team.

Notes

- **Provide pastoral care.**

3. *The* third step.

- **Build strong spiritual foundations.**

    ₪ Build a strong spiritual context for the team to operate in. A revived core will hold the energy to pursue and build with you.

4. *The* fourth step.

- **Have a base from which you operate.**

    ₪ Know your Jerusalem, the place which will be your base.

5. *The* fifth step.

- **Articulate your vision.**

    ₪ Be clear about your vision; what is it you are seeking to achieve?

    ₪ Write your vision out clearly.

- **Ask for help if you are not sure how to present your vision.**

6. *The* sixth step.

- **Bring the team together in prayer.**

    ₪ Reaching out to invite people of goodwill to join you on a prayer journey.

    ₪ The prayer journey should focus on the goals of the first year.

    ₪ The prayer journey relates to the new group you are pioneering.

- **Set clear goals.**

    ₪ If planting a church / congregation / community, a good goal could be about 30 adults.

- **Invite the target community to join you on this adventure into the new.**

    ₪ The invitation should be made out to everyone reachable in the target area.

    ₪ Statisticians say that 8/10 people would like to volunteer and give time to help a socially productive charity.

7. *The* seventh step.

- **Go loud on every success.**

    ₪ Have a culture that celebrates success.

8. *The* eighth step.

- **Pray for the ability to see further.**

    ₪ Set the next clear goals.

    ₪ God is always doing new things, nothing is ever static for too long. This is because God is creative and produces creativity in humanity.

    ₪ The job of leadership is to see beyond the present need and problems, and prepare for the future.

What would be your first year prayer goals?

[B] REVIEW OF THE SESSION

a. The most critical decision you will make is the makeup of your team.

b. Their is no shortcut to building a strong team, it will require effort, time and sacrifice.

c. Jesus saw and selected His own team.

d. The team will need two safe places to grow; a social context to be team and a ministry context to plan strategy.

e. The team will need to understand the vision they are being called to serve and follow.

f. The team will need to go on a pre-launch prayer journey; what does it look like in your context?

g. Believers "overcome by the word of their testimony and the blood of the Lamb", therefore make every testimony large.

h. The core team must be in prayer to receive divine instruction about the future behind the initial goals.

CONCLUSION: WHAT FIVE STEPS DO YOU THINK YOU CAN TAKE TOWARDS ACHIEVING THE BUILDING OF YOUR TEAM?

Notes

NEW WINE SKINS: EXPLORING STRUCTURE

AIMS OF THIS SESSION: IN THIS SESSION WE WILL SEEK TO ENCOURAGE OPENNESS OF THINKING REGARDING STRUCTURES THAT WILL FACILITATE THE BUILDING OF MINISTRY. ORIGINAL THINKING IS A GIFT FROM GOD. WE ARE MADE IN HIS IMAGE AND BRINGING OUR CREATIVITY AND IDEAS INTO SHAPING THE STRUCTURES THAT SUPPORT OUR CALLING IS A GOOD THING.

[A] EMBRACE THE NEW STRUCTURES THAT THE SPIRIT IS TRYING TO INTRODUCE.

1. **Old** practices do not produce new results.

    a. Unless you are persuaded about the new, you will not pursue it.

    b. Unless you are willing to take a risk, you will never step out of your comfort zone.

c. Habits are hard to break.

2. *The* expectation of a new dawn is embedded in the human condition.

a. The cycle of the new day, new year and new moon, is meant to condition us to expect new things.

b. We live in hope for the new.

> *Mark 2:21–22 (NIV) — 21 "No one sews a patch of unshrunk cloth on an old garment. Otherwise, the new piece will pull away from the old, making the tear worse. 22 And no one pours new wine into old wineskins. Otherwise, the wine will burst the skins, and both the wine and the wineskins will be ruined. No, they pour new wine into new wineskins."*

c. Mankind is built to wonder what lies over the horizon.

3. *Jesus* demonstrates the impact of the new in His teaching with authority.

a. Like Jesus, you need to give your vision a teaching context and framework.

> *Mark 1:27 (NIV) — 27 The people were all so amazed that they asked each other, "What is this? A new teaching—and with authority! He even gives orders to impure spirits and they obey him."*

b. Produce a clear narrative that explains how the new will benefit the community you are trying to

Notes

reach.

4. *The* experience of salvation is the personal experience of the new, through a new creative act of God within the human spirit and soul.

    a. God uses the new to introduce what is good for you.

        John 3:3 (NIV) — 3 Jesus replied, "Very truly I tell you, no one can see the kingdom of God unless they are born again."

    b. The new is not limited to a narrow spectrum of life. Expressing itself through new forms of sacramental worship; a new covenant, Heb 9:15 and resulting in a new creation 2 Cor 5:17.

    c. It expresses itself in new ways of thinking.

[B] THE NEW WINESKINS ARE NEW STRUCTURES MEANT TO ACCOMMODATE THE NEW WINE, NOT THE OTHER WAY AROUND.

1. *Ministry* growth.

    a. Ministry will require structures that can cope with and receive that growth.

    b. Have confidence to build what you believe God has called you to build.

    c. It often happens that people inadvertently launch a new ministry as a result of a word from the Lord.

   d. Pioneering out of an expanding
       and growing ministry is both
       challenging and encouraging.

[C] PEOPLE LIVING OUT OF NEW WINE HAVE NEW EXPERIENCES OF THE SPIRIT.

1. **These** new experiences of the Spirit can cause tension in the old structures.

   a. We should nor let tensions stop us
       seeking new experiences of the
       Spirit.

2. **Benefits** of new experiences of the Spirit include:

   a. The impact of the outpouring of
       the new life of the Spirit was so
       great in the New Testament that
       daily conversions took place.

       1 Corinthians 14:24-25 ---
       --- *But if an unbeliever or
       someone who does not
       understand comes in while
       everybody is prophesying,
       he will be convinced by all
       that he is a sinner and will
       be judged by all, {25} and
       the secrets of his heart will
       be laid bare. So he will fall
       down and worship God,
       exclaiming, "God is really
       among you!".*

   b. Scripture shows that conviction
       takes place in the context of the
       presence of the word, the Spirit or
       godly example.

   c. The heart opens up in the
       presence of the saviour.

3. **An** overflowing heart filled with
   worship, praise and love is the result

when the new wine flows, providing three keys to the pioneering of a new community.

    a. Key 1; the facilitation of the ability to maintain momontum.

    b. Key 2; Increased devotion.

    c. Key 3l Clarity of vision.

> *Acts 2:46-47 "Every day they continued to meet together in the temple courts. They broke bread in their homes and ate together with glad and sincere hearts, {47} praising God and enjoying the favour of all the people. And the Lord added to their number daily those who were being saved."*

    d. Momentum was kept because they met daily in the temple courts. The greater the opportunity to have experiences borne out of what God is doing through the new, the greater will be the devotion to the new cause.

[D] TYPES OF CHURCH AND GROUP PIONEERING STRUCTURES FALL INTO MANY CATEGORIES.

1. **A *mother* church plant takes many shapes.**

    a. If pioneering a new church community, explaining how the church came to be involved helps other ministries in the area understand the reason for the pioneering initiative. There is less

Notes

controversy when a new estate opens up, as all ministries in the surrounding area understand the need and the opportunity to plant out a new church or discipleship group.

b. A new church can be established through evangelistic (pioneering individuals).

c. A new church can be established through multiple expressions or congregations of a single church.

d. A new church can be established through a congregational plant (large groups of people planted out into a community).

e. A new church can be established through a multi-campus model.

2. **Ministries and group pioneering fall into many categories.**

a. Unexpected group growth.

b. A new church can be established through discipleship group plant (pioneering group).

c. Hobbies could grow into a new ministry

3. **The greatest difficulties faced by believers in pioneering out, is inflexibility or religion.**

a. Paul was flexible in every cultural context.

Notes

1 Corinthians 9:20–22 (NIV) — 20 "To the Jews I became like a Jew, to win the Jews. To those under the law I became like one under the law (though I myself am not under the law), so as to win those under the law. 21 To those not having the law I became like one not having the law (though I am not free from God's law but am under Christ's law), so as to win those not having the law. 22 To the weak I became weak, to win the weak. I have become all things to all people so that by all possible means I might save some."

   b. We need to learn how to be flexible to the will of the Spirit.

4. *Consider* your pioneering endeavour to be relevant culturally.

   a. Don't believe the hype about the gap between you and those you are trying to reach. The greatest cultural gap that ever existed was between Jesus and the humanity He came to save.

   b. Every church plant will have to work out a structure that facilitates the people the community is trying to reach, and fits into their working and cultural lives.

5. *Consider* how well your structures facilitate team work and development.

   a. Ministry gift trumps office in pioneering.

      ₪ It is essential that a gifting based approach to ministry, rather

Notes

than an office-based approach, is developed.

₪ Don't muddle your anointing with your office.

b. Develop a culture that applauds a team approach.

₪ Be determined to have a team approach to ministry, this is the model Christ gave us.

c. Review current structures. How well do they serve the goals?

d. What is the key goal of structures from a leadership point of view? What purpose should they serve?

[E] THE NEW WINE BROUGHT BY THE SPIRIT MAY BE DESIRED AND WELCOME BUT NEW WINE IS EXPENSIVE.

1. **The** pioneering of any group is going to require finances; planning an affordable model and sticking to it, is essential.

[F] DELEGATING EFFECTIVELY

1. **One** of the skills that a leader will have to learn is the skill of delegating tasks and responsibilities to others.

a. Either delegate to someone you can trust, or do it yourself.

b. Feedback is vital. Leaders must insist on it, 2 Corinthians 4:2.

What skills do you need to develop

2. *There* will be tension.

    a. Tension to manage when pioneering from any sending home church around the fair distribution of resources and skills.

    b. The pioneering pull is seen in the need for resources from those going out.

    c. The apostolic push is seen in the need for sending resources.

    d. The communication gap must be managed.

[G] ACCESSING THE HELP YOU NEED.

1. *Every* pioneering context needs to be connected to a variety of apostolic help.

    • **External help needed includes:**

    a. Help to identify skills deficits.

    b. Help to handle difficult pastoral problems beyond your experience.

    c. Help to identify appropriate leadership development programs should be considered.

[H] REVIEW OF THE SESSION.

    a. Do not be tied to old ways and old structures explore, new ideas.

    b. Jesus demonstrates in His ministry that breakthrough is often predicated on the miraculous.

Notes

c. The Spirit brings order out of chaos; be intentional in allowing Him to breeze through your plans. How would you allow that to happen?

d. The wineskin is meant to accommodate the wine.
The structure is meant to accommodate the vision.

e. Those pioneering with you must be flexible, otherwise the work will fracture before it gets going.

f. Take time to write down the dream before you try and create the structure.

g. Pioneering is about growth; be ruthless in ditching forms that you're not persuaded will produce growth.

Notes

GUIDING THE TEAM

AIMS OF THIS SESSION: IN THIS SESSION WE WILL LOOK AT SOME OF THE PRINCIPLES AROUND BUILDING EFFECTIVE TEAM COLLABORATION, VISION AND IMAGE. ESTABLISHING THE FOUNDATIONS IN THE TEAM ESSENTIALLY SUSTAINS MOMENTUM AND THE ABILITY TO DRIVE FORWARDS THE VISION THAT'S BEEN GIVEN TO YOU BY GOD.

INTRO: a practitioners experience - ask a pioneer to tell you their story of pioneering.

[A] BUILDING TO THE VISION

1. *The* pioneering group is being commissioned to promote a brand.

    a. How would you communicate that message?

    b. The team should be able to communicate the vision easily.

2. *We* need to ensure we communicate a communicable vision.

    a. What do you see as the vision of this new group?

    b. How does the leadership of your community feel about the vision?

    c. What is the pioneered group's relationship to the church vision and how it will be outworked

Notes

Notes

in the group, must be clearly communicable.

Jeremiah 1:11-12 "The word of the LORD came to me "What do you see, Jeremiah?" "I see the branch of an almond tree," I replied. {12} The LORD said to me, "You have seen correctly, for I am watching to see that my word is fulfilled."

d.   What happens if we do not communicate the vision?

Jeremiah 8:6 "I have listened attentively, but they do not say what is right. No one repents of his wickedness, saying, "What have I done?" Each pursues his own course like a horse charging into battle."

e.   If the group vision is not clear, people find their own. This is why being clear about vision is so important.

f.   Vision is the blueprint for building God's Ark in your life.

g.   Abraham's vision gives pointers to where the vision should come from.

Genesis 13:12-17 "Abram lived in the land of Canaan, while Lot lived among the cities of the plain and pitched his tents near Sodom. {13} Now the men of Sodom were wicked and were sinning greatly against the LORD. {14} The LORD said to Abram after Lot had parted from him, "Lift up your eyes from where you arc and look north and south, east and west. {15} All the land that you see I will give to you and your offspring forever. {16} I will make your offspring like the dust of the earth, so that if anyone could count the dust, then your offspring could be counted. {17} Go, walk through the length and breadth of the land, for I am giving it to you."

h. God wanted him to take a good look at the land. God wanted him to become familiar with the land and walk throughout the length of it. Lot chose to go his own way, but Abraham waited upon God's direction.

3. *Teaching* alignment is critical to success.

a. The team needs to be taught the value and benefit of working as one.

b. The assignment requires alignment.

₪ A communal cup demands a communal vision!

₪ Coca Cola mixed with tea tastes awful. A mixed up vision produces;

i. Confusion.

ii.   Mixed messages.

iii. Mixed priorities.

c.   Be clear about your core values, as it affects your ability to shape the culture within which you are all working.

[B] PASTORING HOPES

1. *Every* individual in the team have personal preferences and individual hopes.

   a.   A clear vision helps individuals understand how they play a part

2. *Extend* and appropriately open up leadership to the core group.

   a.   You are there to provide pastoral care for the sheep, this includes their hopes and dreams.

   b.   A scattering of the sheep comes about as a result of the lack of a shepherd.

   Ezekiel 34:5 "So they were scattered because there was no shepherd, and when they were scattered they became food for all the wild animals."

   c.   True shepherds know the condition of every sheep in the group.

   Proverbs 27:23 "Be sure you know the condition of your flocks, give careful attention to your herds".

d. The sheep will rightly begin to lean on the leaders and require help and support.

John 21:17 "The third time he said to him, "Simon son of John, do you love me?" Peter was hurt because Jesus asked him the third time, "Do you love me?" He said, "Lord, you know all things; you know that I love you. " Jesus said, "Feed my sheep."

[C] BROKEN CISTERNS CAN BE REPAIRED.

1. **Consider** how to help individuals who are carrying hurts from the past.

    a. Christ ministers liberty to us so that we can serve - Hebrews 9:11-15 (NIV).

    b. Cultivate a repentant culture.

    Acts 3:19-21 (NIV) "Repent, then, and turn to God, so that your sins may be wiped out, that times of refreshing may come from the Lord, [20] and that he may send the Christ, who has been appointed for you—even Jesus. [21] He must remain in heaven until the time comes for God to restore everything, as he promised long ago through his holy prophets. Insecurities in present leaders will hinder a change to more dynamic form of ministry and church expression."

    c. We all need to be healed from past

Notes

hurts, and everyone needs a right perspective about themselves.

1 Corinthians 12:7-9 "Now to each one the manifestation of the Spirit is given for the common good. {8} To one there is given through the Spirit the message of wisdom, to another the message of knowledge by means of the same Spirit, {9} to another faith by the same Spirit, to another gifts of healing by that one Spirit,"

d. When God fills us with the Holy Spirit He equips every single one of us.

e. "Every member of the team will need a shift in their personal perspective. The Lords perspective was different to Gideon's perspective of himself.

Judges 6:11-19 The angel of the LORD came and sat down under the oak in Ophrah that belonged to Joash the Abiezrite, where his son Gideon was threshing wheat in a winepress to keep it from the Midianites. {12} When the angel of the LORD appeared to Gideon, he said, "The LORD is with you, mighty warrior." {13} "But sir," Gideon replied, "if the LORD is with us, why has all this happened to us? Where are all his wonders that our fathers told us about when they said, `Did not the LORD

Notes

*bring us up out of Egypt?'
But now the LORD has
abandoned us and put us
into the hand of Midian."
{14} The LORD turned to
him and said, "Go in the
strength you have and
save Israel out of Midian's
hand. Am I not sending
you?" {15} "But Lord,"
Gideon asked, "how can I
save Israel? My clan is the
weakest in Manasseh, and
I am the least in my family."
{16} The LORD answered,
"I will be with you, and
you will strike down all the
Midianites together." {17}
Gideon replied, "If now I
have found favour in your
eyes, give me a sign that
it is really you talking to
me. {18} Please do not
go away until I come back
and bring my offering and
set it before you." And the
LORD said, "I will wait until
you return." {19} Gideon
went in, prepared a young
goat, and from an ephah
of flour he made bread
without yeast. Putting the
meat in a basket and its
broth in a pot, he brought
them out and offered them
to him under the oak."*

2. *Helping* the team build a right self-image.

a.   We derive our image from God.

₪ In building up our self-image, we need to recognise that we are weak vessels who can do nothing that will count for eternity without God's help.

Notes

₪ *2 Corinthians 12:10 "That is why, for Christ's sake, I delight in weaknesses, in insults, in hardships, in persecutions, in difficulties. For when I am weak, then I am strong. " (C/f) Colossians 2:8 See to it that no one takes you captive through hollow and deceptive philosophy, which depends on human tradition and the basic principles of this world rather than on Christ."*

b.　We are part of the most amazing family in the world.

> *John 1:12-13　"Yet to all who received him, to those who believed in his name, he gave the right to become children of God-- {13} children born not of natural descent, nor of human decision or a husband's will, but born of God."*

c.　Our weakness only masks His divine power that dwells in us.

> *2 Peter 1:3　"His divine power has given us everything we need for life and godliness through our knowledge of him who called us by his own glory and goodness."*

> *2 Corinthians 4:7　"But we have this treasure in jars of clay to show that this all-surpassing power is from God and not from us."*

₪　We have a competency that comes from Christ.

2 Corinthians 3:4-6 "Such confidence as this is ours through Christ before God. {5} Not that we are competent in ourselves to claim anything for ourselves, but our competence comes from God. {6} He has made us competent as ministers of a new covenant-not of the letter but of the Spirit; for the letter kills, but the Spirit gives life."

d. Whatever we were, we have acquired a new status; that of royalty.

    1 Peter 2:9   "But you are a chosen people, a royal priesthood, a holy nation, a people belonging to God, that you may declare the praises of him who called you out of darkness into his wonderful light."

[D] PLANNED MOMENTUM

1. **KEY** INSIGHT: Don't lose it by chopping and changing.

    a. Stick to your vision.

    b. Be cognisant of seasonal changes that affect the flow of planned momentum. For example every church is affected to some degree by the summer exodus of people leaving church to go on holiday or visit Christian camps.

        Colossians   2:2   "My purpose is that they may be encouraged in heart and united in love, so that they may have the full riches of complete understanding, in order that they may know the mystery of God, namely, Christ,"

2 Corinthians 1:6 "If we are distressed, it is for your comfort and salvation; if we are comforted, it is for your comfort, which produces in you patient endurance of the same sufferings we suffer."

[E]. KILLING RELIGION IN

DISCIPLESHIP

1. **The** pursuit of grace whilst holding people to account, is essential to personal growth.

2. **An** environment of mercy whilst holding on to discipline and honestly challenging each other, is vital to genuine discipleship and growth.

[H] REVIEW OF THE SESSION

a. Building a team is like building anything; you consider the foundations, the infrastructure, the purpose and what it is serving.

b. What is the team's identity; is it a kingdom team or a secularly driven team?

c. What is the brand and how is that being communicated? Use simple steps to communicate rather than elaborate.

d. What is your vision?

e. How do you intend to deploy

Notes

members of the core team?

f.   Why are individuals joining your team, do you really know what motivates them?

g.   How do you plan to maintain momentum?

Notes

NEW WINE RESULTS IN A NEW CULTURE

AIMS OF THIS SESSION: IN THIS SESSION WE WILL CONSIDER HOW CULTURE AFFECTS THE WAY THE TEAM IMPACTS ON THE COMMUNITY IT IS TRYING TO REACH. THE TEAM CULTURE FORMS THE MICRO-CLIMATE FROM WHICH THOSE WHO CONNECT WITH THE MINISTRY OF PIONEERING TEAM BENEFIT. IT FORMS A VISUAL TESTIMONY OF THE FRUIT OF THE MINISTRY.

Keys to a Cultural Shift

[A] YOU CAN'T CHANGE THE COMMUNITY IF YOU HAVE NOT CHANGED YOUR CULTURE.

1. *It's* not what you know that counts in setting the culture of the pioneered community or ministry.

   a. Cultural change does not necessarily come because of knowledge; for example the five big cause of ill health in the UK are all reversible. Ultimately depending on their continued grip on an individual through free will.

b. History teaches us that change comes because someone is desperate.

2. *A prophetic* culture is strongly influenced by the pursuit of renewal.

a. What is spiritual excellence?

b. Excellence is, that which is commonly regarded as excellent; in arts, letters, manners, scholarly pursuits, etc.

c. Excellence is, a particular form or stage of civilization.

d. Excellence is, demonstrated in what is aspired to by a social, ethnic, or particular age group. It is transmitted from one generation to another.

e. Whatever is perceived as excellent in culture is what everyone strives for.

3. *We* change the culture by nurturing a heavenly mindset.

a. Our citizenship is in heaven.

Colossians 3:1–4 (NIV) — *1 "Since, then, you have been raised with Christ, set your hearts on things above, where Christ is, seated at the right hand of God. 2 Set your minds on things above, not on earthly things. 3 For you died, and your life is now hidden with Christ in God. 4 When Christ, who is your life, appears, then you also will appear with him in glory."*

Notes

b. Store up for yourselves treasure in heaven and avoid an over reliance on worldly wisdom.

1 Corinthians 3:19 (NIV) *"For the wisdom of this world is foolishness in God's sight. As it is written: "He catches the wise in their craftiness"*

4. *How* do we nurture a heavenly mindset so that our culture can change?

a. A culture of renewal is facilitated through pursuit of relationship with our Father in heaven

Matthew 6:9-10 *"This, then, is how you should pray: "'Our Father in heaven, hallowed be your name, [10] your kingdom come,"*

b. Renewal is;

"The intentional, focused, determined but tender pursuit of intimate relationship with our Father through His Son and by His Spirit." - Yinka Oyekan

c. We nurture this heavenly mindset, understanding it subsequently leads to a prophetic culture.

₪ It becomes prophetic because it brings with it the desire to see and hear the will of the Father revealed and outworked on earth.

5. **W**e nurture a heavenly mindset by encouraging ourselves to expect the miraculous.

 a. A culture of renewal produces the expectation of supernatural restoration. When John the Baptist suffered a crisis of faith, Jesus pointed to the environment that surrounded Him, producing hope.

 Matthew 11:5-14 (NIV) [5] "The blind receive sight, the lame walk, those who have leprosy are cured, the deaf hear, the dead are raised, and the good news is preached to the poor."

 b. Isa 61 shows that the anointing is the key central source of sustained community transformation and precedes the outworking of ministry.

 c. Through the anointing, barren places become blossoming fields.

 Isaiah 35:1-4 "The desert and the parched land will be glad; the wilderness will rejoice and blossom. Like the crocus, [2] it will burst into bloom; it will rejoice greatly and shout for joy. The glory of Lebanon will be given to it, the splendour of Carmel and Sharon; they will see the glory of the LORD, the splendour of our God. [3] Strengthen the feeble hands, steady the knees that give way; [4] say to those with fearful hearts, "Be strong, do not fear; your God will come, he will come with vengeance; with divine retribution he will come to save you."

d. We nurture this mindset by reminding ourselves that with the new wine of renewal, comes a change in the environment.

ℶ A change in environment that brings healing is seen with the woman with the issue of blood and it is seen with blind Bartemaeus.

ℶ A transformation in those who exist in this environment is evident. The disciples after three years living in the presence of Jesus carried the same grace of healing and restoration that He did.

ℶ They are seen to be healing the sick such; as the healing of the crippled beggar at the Beautiful Gate Acts 3:1-10.

ℶ People were astonished at faith that made the beggar well Acts 3:16.

e. The change in mindset leads to a willingness to let the Lord change the heart. The restoration of the world starts with renewal of the heart.

6. *Practically,* a prophetic culture is bound to see and must lead to a change in structures.

a. As the new is pursued, it will lead to an understanding of changes that are required to make things work.

b. How to discern spiritual restoration.

ℶ It originates in a new and personal hunger after God.

c. Spiritual renewal and ministry is at root concerned about the spiritual well-being of the other and not just their physical well being. It is spiritually concerned and not just practically concerned.

d. It always makes Christ known as the reason for restoration.

7. *However* renewal looks, it starts in the heart.

> *1 Peter 3:15* (NIV) *"But in your hearts set apart Christ as Lord. Always be prepared to give an answer to everyone who asks you to give the reason for the hope that you have. But do this with gentleness and respect"*

8. *To* maintain a freshness in the culture, keep the new wine flowing.

a. Maintaining a culture of renewal is like planting a tree beside a river.

b. Such a culture accesses the river flowing from God's Temple Ezekiel 47:1-12

₪ Joel had mentioned this river. Joel 3:18 (NIV), as did Zechariah after the Babylonian Captivity (cf. Zechariah 14:8 (NIV)

₪ The River flowing from the temple made the dead Sea which is six times saltier than the ocean, completely salt-free—so that where the river flows everything will live.

Notes

c. These waters signify the gospel of Christ.

[B] THE NEW WINE IS MAINTAINED AND FACILITATED IN THE COMMUNITY BY;

1. **The** pursuit of prayer.

    a. Make prayer your personal priority.

    b. We can only pass on what we have received.

    c. Bringing heaven down as an intentional lifestyle.

2. **Integrity** : Learning to lead through authentic example.

    • **Transparent leaders.**

        ₪ When a leader makes himself vulnerable and open, and where leaders share heart; making internal struggles accessible whilst honestly sharing failures as well as successes, the people following will be able to trust, and in turn open up.

        ₪ Tithing should be a clear discipline practiced by leaders.

        ₪ Commitment to key community gatherings should be a discipline practiced by leaders.

3. **Create** space for testimonies.

    a. You give your time to what you believe in.

Notes

b. You give time to those you love.

c. Encourage the maintenance of testimonies.

d. Live in the fruit God produces, not your failures.

4. **Renewal brings people into an environment of peace, joy and belonging.**

a. The target group are reaching out to people who need to feel welcome.

b. The individual is more important than the program.

c. Everyone needs a listening ear.

5. **The growing group needs to remain an open group.**

a. While the group begins to get together, being clear how it intends to remain open to interested outsiders into the group will be hard work.

b. One of the disciplines required to remain an open group will be the discipline of maintaining a lifestyle of sharing the gospel. Going fishing for souls requires going the extra mile.

Luke 5:4-7 *"When he had finished speaking, he said to Simon, "Put out into deep water, and let down the nets for a catch. " {5} Simon answered, "Master, we've worked hard all night and haven't caught anything. But because you say so, I will let down the nets. " {6} When they had*

Notes

done so, they caught such a large number of fish that their nets began to break. {7} So they signalled their partners in the other boat to come and help them, and they came and filled both boats so full that they began to sink."

c. Sometimes drawing the target group into the discipleship group will entail a lot of toil for what appears to be little fruit.

Galatians 6:9 "Let us not become weary in doing good, for at the proper time we will reap a harvest if we do not give up. (C/f) 1 Corinthians 15:58 Therefore, my dear brothers, stand firm. Let nothing move you. Always give yourselves fully to the work of the Lord, because you know that your labour in the Lord is not in vain."

[C] HOW DO WE AVOID WEARINESS?

1. **We** should not allow ourselves to become tired in pioneering.

   2 Thessalonians 3:13 "And as for you, brothers, never tire of doing what is right."

   a. We should not become tired of doing good.

   Proverbs 3:27 "Do not withhold good from those who deserve it, when it is in your power to act." (C/f) Romans 12:13 "Share with God's people who are in need. Practice hospitality."

Notes

b. The core group needs to familiarise itself with the problems of its target group; for instance, a group interested in single parents will need to know the daily problems single parents face. Armed with such understanding, the group is better able to relate and be relevant to them.

[D] AWARENESS OF THOSE WHO ARE MISSING FROM A MEETING IS AS IMPORTANT AS THOSE WHO MAKE IT.

1. **Face** the problem of disengagement and why people stop coming to the group.

   a. There is always a reason people stop attending the group.

   b. A group mentality that cares about individuals who are missing makes for stronger bonds. We must learn to care about group members that do not turn up, as well as those who are responding to the group evangelistic efforts.

   Luke 15:4 *"Suppose one of you has a hundred sheep and loses one of them. Does he not leave the ninety-nine in the open country and go after the lost sheep until he finds it?" (c/f)* *1 Peter 2:25* *"For you were like sheep going astray, but now you have returned to the Shepherd and Overseer of your souls."*

2. **God's** heart is for His lost sheep.

   Ezekiel 34:11-16 *"'For this is what the Sovereign LORD says I myself will*

Notes

search for my sheep and look after them. {12} As a shepherd looks after his scattered flock when he is with them, so will I look after my sheep. I will rescue them from all the places where they were scattered on a day of clouds and darkness. {13} I will bring them out from the nations and gather them from the countries, and I will bring them into their own land. I will pasture them on the mountains of Israel, in the ravines and in all the settlements in the land. {14} I will tend them in a good pasture, and the mountain heights of Israel will be their grazing land. There they will lie down in good grazing land, and there they will feed in a rich pasture on the mountains of Israel. {15} I myself will tend my sheep and have them lie down, declares the Sovereign LORD. {16} I will search for the lost and bring back the strays. I will bind up the injured and strengthen the weak, but the sleek and the strong I will destroy. I will shepherd the flock with justice."

John 10:11-14 "I am the good shepherd. The good shepherd lays down his life for the sheep. {12} The hired hand is not the shepherd who owns the sheep. So when he sees the wolf coming, he abandons the sheep and runs away. Then the

Notes

wolf attacks the flock and scatters it. {13} The man runs away because he is a hired hand and cares nothing for the sheep. {14} "I am the good shepherd; I know my sheep and my sheep know me"

a. Developing a means of keeping a tab on those who do not come is therefore important. Can, you suggest four ways to do this? Which of these do you think is best and why?

b. Whatever the reason they need adequate pastoral care and we have to ensure that they get it, if they want or need it. We need to avoid assuming why people do not come.

c. We must not take offence when people fail to do a simple thing like telephone to explain why they are absent. Sometimes people don't phone to explain their absence because they just do not want to trouble us.

[E] REVIEW OF THE SESSION.

a. Culture eats values and theology for breakfast.

b. The importation of information is not the same thing as acquisition of knowledge.

c. Promote insight into the culture of heaven wherever you can; it draws the mind above and beyond the parochial.

Notes

d. The facilitation of a deeper relationship with the Father strengthens a relational culture on earth, because the Father's love for humanity draws the human heart into relationship with the other.

e. Developing a system of keeping in touch with respondents is essential.

f. Proactive pursuit of renewal enables the maintenance of every ministry dream.

Notes

PRODUCING A CULTURE OF ADVENTURE

AIMS OF THIS SESSION: IN THIS SESSION WE WILL CONSIDER PRINCIPLES THAT HELP TO MAINTAIN FAITH, AND TO ENCOURAGE FAITHFULNESS IN THE TEAM THAT'S WORKING WITH YOU.

WE USE THE LORD'S PRAYER AS A TEMPLATE FOR LEARNING ABOUT PRAYER, WE WILL USE THE TEACHING ON 'INREACH', A SYNONYM FOR JESUS' EVANGELISTIC PROGRAM AS A TEMPLATE AND A FRAMEWORK FOR LEARNING ABOUT HOW MINISTRY CAN REPLICATE ITSELF.

1. *It* is the Spirit who produces a call and direction, he is the adventure maker, thus remaining sensitive to the spirit is a discipline to be developed.

2. *Producing* faith in the group is the responsibility of everyone in the group or community.

   a. Every church group, whatever the specific reason for gathering, should be outward looking.

   b. How is multiplication viewed?

      ₪ We must encourage the group to have a sense of mission and belief that they have the authority in Christ to accomplish group goals. Matthew 9:35-10:1.

      ₪ The group must have a clear sense of the people they are targeting. Matthew 10:5.

   c. Have a "harvest is ready now" mentality. John 4:31-36.

   d. Faith for the harvest is essential.

      ₪ We can do greater things John 14:12.

      ₪ We function just as the Son did John 5:19.

      ₪ To generate faith you must have faith. Matthew 21:21.

      ₪ Genuine faith has feet, the discipleship group must be willing to go to the people they are trying to reach. Isaiah 52:7.

e. The group needs to be
    encouraged to put their ideas into
    practice. James 2:18

    ₪ All the theoretical words or
    teaching in the world will not make
    up for one literal step taken in love
    towards the lost.

    ₪ You can catch someone's faith
    for evangelism, it is something that
    is infectious.

    Romans 1:11-12 *"I long to
    see you so that I may impart
    to you some spiritual gift
    to make you strong-- {12}
    that is, that you and I may
    be mutually encouraged
    by each other's faith."*

f. An introverted group becomes
    blind.

g. As the group meets, it needs
    to keep its perspective
    heavenwards.

h. Foster genuine faith towards the
    prophetic words received.

    Psalms 119:36 *"Turn my
    heart toward your statutes
    and not toward selfish
    gain."*

i. Don't be distracted by trends,
    fashions or immediate needs Luke
    10:40.

Notes

3. *Faith* is tenacious.

a. Genuine faith is determined. 2 Timothy 4:5.

b. Genuine faith is focused despite difficulties. Paul was qualified to say these things. 2 Corinthians 11:23-33.

c. Faith is determined and so it can be described as termed vision. It fits into a time frame.

d. Although it has a long term perspective, it also embraces short term goals, such as Philip did in Samaria. Acts 8:4-8.

e. Faith has passion. Not the short termism of the one whom received the word with joy, only to melt away under the first bit of pressure.

f. Explore and encourage evangelistic ideas that originate both within and outside the group.

g. Individuals with a burning evangelistic heart are given to the church in order to grow the church.

Ephesians 4:11-12 "It was he who gave some to be apostles, some to be prophets, some to be evangelists, and some to be pastors and teachers, {12} to prepare God's people for works of service, so that the body of Christ may be built up."

Notes

h. Genuine faith needs to be encouraged and released into the group through stories of how others have accomplished God's given vision. The group needs to seed itself in how others did it.

Hebrews 12:1 *"Therefore, since we are surrounded by such a great cloud of witnesses, let us throw off everything that hinders and the sin that so easily entangles, and let us run with perseverance the race marked out for us."*

₪ People like Wigglesworth, Hudson Taylor and Mary Slessor are good examples that provoke faith.

i. Be open to creative methods of reaching the lost in your area. Nobody will want to argue much with results.

j. Help them overcome the negative fears they have.

₪ How have people in the past put individuals in the group off?

2 Corinthians 10:5 *"We demolish arguments and every pretension that sets itself up against the knowledge of God, and we take captive every thought to make it obedient to Christ."*

₪ These negative ideas become strongholds in the mind, which bind and hinder service and expectancy.

» These negative ideas become shared ideas in the group. If they are not dealt with they will hinder the group itself.

» There is nothing that can stop a group, except the will of God.

k. Your group can't burn on its own, you will need encouragement. Jesus sent them out in two's. All the members of the discipleship group need to be mobilised. Caring becomes impossible for just one couple to handle as the group grows. This will either lead to delegating pastoral care to others, or a cutting back by discipleship group leaders.

Matthew 9:37-38 "Then he said to his disciples, "The harvest is plentiful but the workers are few. {38} Ask the Lord of the harvest, therefore, to send out workers into his harvest field."

4. ***Inreach* - Jesus' core evangelistic strategy. The principles gleaned from Inreach, Jesus evangelistic program, will work as a template for considering how to build up a ministry.**

   • **Principle one. Jesus calls us to ministry that creates disciples in the context of serving.**

   a. We need a strategy for making disciples of people and a programme of teaching them.

   b. Jesus wants us to make disciples, that make disciples. Obey Him or you will be run off your feet.

Matthew   28:19-20
Therefore go and make disciples of all nations, baptising them in the name of the Father and of the Son and of the Holy Spirit, {20} and teaching them to obey everything I have commanded you. And surely I am with you always, to the very end of the age."

c.   Where does Inreach come from?

₪ When Jesus sent out His disciples He did not just tell them to have outreach (Matthew 10:11-13), He also encouraged them to find a home that would welcome them and out of relationship, try to reach that town or village. It was important to reach the community by reaching individuals. This is why we use the term INREACH.

₪ *Matthew 10:7- 13   "As you go, preach this message 'The kingdom of heaven is near. ' {8} Heal the sick, raise the dead, cleanse those who have leprosy, drive out demons. Freely you have received, freely give. {9} Do not take along any gold or silver or copper in your belts; {10} take no bag for the journey, or extra tunic, or sandals or a staff; for the worker is worth his keep. {11} "Whatever town or village you enter, search for some worthy person there and stay at his house until you leave. {12} As you enter the home, give it your greeting. {13} If the home is deserving, let your peace rest on it; if it is not, let your peace return to you."*

Notes

- **Principle two. Jesus wants us to build genuine relationships with the people we are trying to reach.**

  d. Outreach without Inreach is incomplete evangelism, Jesus expects both from us.

- **Principle three. We need to work out how we can be invited into the social circles of those we are trying to reach, so that we become part of their lives. The kind of events that facilitate evangelistic social integration 'Inreach' events, will work for almost any ministry.**

  ₪ The question is, how in this generation can we place ourselves in such a position that strangers would welcome us into their home? The solution is found in a list of "Inreach events".

  ₪   Inreach is a strategic means of drawing the targeted people into a form of discipleship.

  ₪ It has as its goal, the building of relationships.

  ₪ The discipleship group will have to be honest about forms of pioneering or evangelism it has tried, that have worked or have failed. Such honesty is challenging.

  ₪   Jesus said if you face the truth it will set you free.

  ₪ Picture the scene. A husband and wife go out shopping, the wife spots a lovely dress and decides to try it on. This is the fifth dress she has tried on. She comes out of the booth excited and asks her husband "what do you think". He is afraid to tell her the truth in case she gets upset. Eventually he does. They get home that evening and his wife cooks a new type of meal. It is absolutely dreadful, but his wife is waiting for his approving nod. He knows that if he lies he will have to eat this for the rest of his life. But he also does not want to disappoint her any further on that particular day. What should he do?

  e.   If we do not face the facts about our pioneering or evangelistic efforts then we will never change our approach.

  f.   An "Inreach" event is an event that takes place in or around the host's house. The events could consist of some of the following.

  ₪ An "Inreach" could be a meal. Meals from around the world would be a wonderful draw.

  ₪ An "Inreach" could consist of a games evening. Trivial Pursuit or other board games would be helpful. Going out for a meal with a neighbour is also a means of reaching them, it can end up with coffee back at home. But why the stress on going back home after a night out? If a neighbour will have you into their home or come into yours, it means there is an openness and trust which can be built upon.

₪ Outdoor events which then end up back at the home of the Christian include things like visits to the Theatre, Cinema, Opera, or Zoo.

₪ Sporting activities, or events, such as five aside football, badminton, volleyball can also lead to Inreach.

₪ The idea of Inreach is to help the group learn to develop a series of close meaningful friendships. Most Christians have got few non-Christian friends and have lost the ability to build friendships with non-Christians.

₪ What is a friend? It is not an acquaintance which is what most Christians instantly assume it to mean. An acquaintance or work colleague, is not a friend, if in fact the only reason you see them or spend time with them is because you have to work with them. A friend is someone whom you choose to and want to, spend your free time with.

₪ In the group identify those with a particularly strong evangelistic heart and use them to help encourage the group in Inreach.

₪ The group will need to lean on every gifting regardless of whether it is strongly evangelistic or not. You can't build a house with only electricians, somewhere along the line you will need builders, roofers, plumbers and other skilled work-ers.

g. The purpose of identifying those with a pioneering or evangelistic heart, is that they can help in the preparation of an ongoing list of "Inreach" events, which should receive contributions from group members. Where appropriate, it is a good idea to share this information with other discipleship groups in the church.

₪ 90% of people who are saved, are saved because a family mem-ber or friend took time to love and befriend them, and by such means provide a platform for the recep-tion of the gospel. While only 10% of people who are in church are saved through simply going to a meeting without any contact. Why not do a quick survey of your disci-pleship group and see how many came to Christ through being befriended, or helped by a family member.

5. *The* cost of Inreach.

*   **Principle four. To build any ministry that reaches people will have a cost attached to it, to be successful everyone in the core team must be willing to pay the price.**

    a. Inreach costs time. Certainly the individual family units and in some cases where appropriate, church groups e.g. (ladies group) would have to give up one evening a week to practice "Inreach"

    ₪ Inreach costs because it

Notes

demands a greater degree of accountability from members. Accountability in the "Inreach" programme, will be best done through a system of "reporting back".

b. Most people accept the need for accountability for their Christian walk.

₪ The idea of being accountable for our pioneering or evangelistic efforts might not immediately sit well with individuals, especially if a heavy handed approach is adopted. But, if accountability through encouragement is the emphasis, then people will embrace it wholeheartedly.

- **Principle five. Regular feedback on progress is essential for maintaining momentum.**

    ₪ Nevertheless Jesus made His disciples accountable for their pioneering or evangelistic efforts, and when they returned, they gave a report of what happened when they were away.

    Luke 9:10 "When the apostles returned, they reported to Jesus what they had done. Then he took them with him and they withdrew by themselves to a town called Bethsaida,

(C/f) Luke 10:17-19 "The seventy-two returned with joy and said, "Lord, even the demons submit to us in your name." {18} He replied, "I saw Satan fall like lightning from heaven. {19} I have given you authority to trample on snakes and scorpions and to overcome all the power of the enemy; nothing will harm you."

(C/f)   Luke 9:10 "When the apostles returned, they reported to Jesus what they had done. Then he took them with him and they withdrew by themselves to a town called Bethsaida,

₪ Individuals can "report-back", outlining how the Inreach attempt has fared that week. This way the benefits and pitfalls can be shared and learned. The shape and purpose of church life in the discipleship group need not be affected, "reporting back" need only take a few moments and ideas and tips can be exchanged.

₪ Accountability could also be undertaken in the other various appropriate church groups (e.g.) youth group (etc.).

₪ Sharing information is vital to encourage the church. The discipleship group should consider how best to keep the church informed. On Sundays there should be updates on how things are going, who has been saved etc.

Notes

[E] MEASURING SUCCESS

1. We measure success by how deeply our cultures are rooted in our teams .

2. Success is evident where failure is acknowledged but still celebrated and praised

3. Life is dynamically and organically growing and failure does not pull the team to a halt.

4. Team members are living in renewal.

LIST HOW THE FIVE PRINCIPLES GLEANED FROM 'INREACH' COULD AFFECT YOUR CURRENT MINISTRY.

[F] REVIEW OF THE SESSION

a. Encouraging tenacity with faith produces miracles.

b. Pioneering objectives have to be clear. Who is it that has to be reached? This helps us to be clear who it is we should invest social time with.

c. Consider the impact of leaders who prayed a lot.

d. Good preaching is central.

e. Everyone has a role to play.

Notes

THE RELATIONSHIP OF SACRIFICE TO GROWTH

AIMS OF THIS SESSION: IN THIS SESSION WE WILL CONSIDER AND EXPLORE THE KIND OF SACRIFICES THAT WE MUST BE WILLING TO MAKE IN ORDER TO ACHIEVE OUR VISION.

Intro: A practitioner's experience. Ask a pioneer to explain their experience of how sacrifice and growth are related and impact upon one another.

[A] PAYING THE PRICE REQUIRED FOR THE ANOINTING)

1. **The** cost is great;

   a. If you are called of God then the group leadership is part of God's plan for your life. Your faithfulness to it, is in reality, faithfulness to people.

      Luke 16:10-13 *"Whoever can be trusted with very little can also be trusted with much, and whoever is dishonest with very little will also be dishonest with much. 11 So if you have not been trustworthy in handling worldly wealth, who will trust you with true riches? 12 And if you have not been trustworthy with someone else's property, who will give you property of your own? 13 "No servant can serve two masters. Either he will hate the one and love the other, or he will be devoted to the one and despise the other. You cannot serve both God and Money."*

[B] SHOULD I EXPECT A RETURN?

2. **The** facts are that every investor expects a return;

   a. Banks want a return on loans.

   b. Shareholders want a return on shares bought.

   c. Savers want a return on their savings.

3. **Jesus** said "I will build my church."

   a. Because Jesus intends to build His church you can expect Him to help you with your ministry.

   KEY INSIGHT: **How does He build His church?**

[C] THE INTEGRATION OF PEOPLE TO LIFE.

4. **The** integration of people groups into church life will present the biggest challenge to this generation.

   a. The reason is simple, society continues to fragment in many ways.

   b. Individual's personal lives also tend to be fractured, with many people having to work in two jobs just to provide for their families.

   c. Reaching fragmented people groups then will become a vital area of focus for the church. Specialised, dedicated and focused groups could provide a meeting point for the fragmented communities we find ourselves living in.

Notes

STRENGTHENING THE RELATIONAL CULTURE

AIMS OF THIS SESSION: CULTURE EATS OUR BELIEFS AND VISION FOR BREAKFAST. IN THE SESSION WE WILL LOOK AT AND EXPLORE THE IMPACT THAT CULTURE CAN HAVE ON THE EFFECTIVENESS OF A TEAM SEEKING TO PIONEER A GROUP, MINISTRY OR CHURCH.

1. **A Serving culture.**

   a. Jesus came to serve not to be served Matthew 20:20-28 (NIV)

   b. Real freedom results in servanthood Galatians 5:1-14 (NIV)

   c. True godly leadership is servant leadership 1 Peter 5:1-8 (NIV)

   d. Each should use whatever gift he has to serve 1 Peter 4:7-11 (NIV)

   e. What is a culture of serving? It is, " the facilitating, stewarding, and enabling of loving relationships which mirror the intimacy we have with our Father. The giving of ourselves in acts of love.

2. **A Relational culture.**

   a. Christ constantly seeks a relational heart.

      Revelation 3:19-22 (NIV) [19] "Those whom I love I rebuke and discipline. So be earnest, and repent. [20] Here I am! I stand at the door and knock. If anyone hears my voice and opens the door, I will come in and eat with him, and he with me. 21] To him who overcomes, I will give the right to sit with me on my throne, just as I overcame and sat down with my Father on his throne. [22] He who has an ear, let him hear what the Spirit says to the churches."

   b. To be a father or mother is not just a biological function.

   c. How does one father nations? Genesis 17:4-6 (NIV)

      ₪ He was a father by example of faith. Romans 4:13-17.

      ₪ God's promise to your family will be fulfilled.

₪ God's promise to Abraham saying "I will make you a great nation," fulfilled:

    i.   It was fulfilled by God creating the Hebrew people (Ge 13:16 , Jn 8:37).

    ii. It was also spiritually fulfilled (Jn 8:39; Ro 4:16; Ga 3:6-7,29), (Ge 17:18-20).

    iii. It was fulfilled in that God made Abraham's name great. Not just in Judaism but in all three great world religions—Judaism, Islam, and Christianity.

    iv. The promise to Abraham that all nations on earth would be blessed through him was fulfilled by God through the Messiah - "In you all the families of the earth shall be blessed." (Jn 8:56-58; Ga 3:16).

d. In relationships, what are the spiritual responsibilities of a son or daughter?

e. Christians have a spirit of sonship.

    ₪ We are all sons and daughters of God.

    ₪ We cry Abba Father.

    ₪ Living in intimacy.

Notes

f. Dysfunctional people will need healing.

₪ Dysfunction is seen in sons like David, with fathers like Saul.

₪ Dysfunction is seen in fathers like David with sons like Absalom.

₪ Dysfunction is seen in an orphaned Spirit which always questions identity.

g. Wholeness is seen in;

₪ Mothers like Mary.

₪ The Generous Father & the Prodigal Son who repositioned himself.

₪ Sweetest of relationships; David and Jonathan.

h. A relational culture grows through honour

₪ In our nation, dishonour is seen as acceptable.

₪ Is honour something we should seek and want?

₪ *Romans 2:6-10 (NIV) God "will give to each person according to what he has done." [7] To those who by persistence in doing good seek glory, honour and immortality, he will give eternal life. [8] But for those who are self-seeking and who reject the truth and follow evil, there will be wrath and anger. [9] There will be trouble and distress for every human being who does evil: first for the Jew, then for the Gentile; [10] but glory, honour*

Notes

and peace for everyone who does good: first for the Jew, then for the Gentile.

i.   Honour is not just for the good and the great.

   » Angels (scripture below) refuse to speak slanderously – it is not the culture of heaven – they err on the side of honour Jude 3-9 (NIV).

   » The differences in creation between a man and a woman is an occasion for honour – men are generally physically stronger.

j.   Parents are to be honoured

   Exodus 20:12 (NIV) "Honour your father and your mother, so that you may live long in the land the LORD your God is giving you.

k.   Honour is a relational gift in which I chose to speak well of, and treat with dignity my brother, sister, mother and father.

l.   Honour given draws the best out of us.

m. Honour given provides an environment in which we can prosper.

n.   Relational culture starts in the home.

Notes

o. The home is meant to be a reflection of heaven.

p. God is to be honoured, Revelation 5:13 (NIV).

q. Leaders are to be honoured - 1 Timothy 5:17 (NIV) .

r. Why people withhold honour.

s. Fathers and mothers produce after their own kind.

t. Every thing has a father, for example scripture talks about the Father of those who play instruments etc.

> *Follow me as I follow Christ 1 Corinthians 11:1 (NIV) Follow my example, as I follow the example of Christ.*

3. *A Culture of Learning.*

a. Teaching each other comes out of the context of a worshipping heart.

> *Colossians 3:1-17 (NIV) [3:1] "Since, then, you have been raised with Christ, set your hearts on things above, where Christ is seated at the right hand of God. [2] Set your minds on things above, not on earthly things. [3] For you died, and your life is now hidden with Christ in God. [4] When Christ, who is your life, appears, then you also will appear with him in glory.*

Notes

[5] Put to death, therefore, whatever belongs to your earthly nature: sexual immorality, impurity, lust, evil desires and greed, which is idolatry. [6] Because of these, the wrath of God is coming. [7] You used to walk in these ways, in the life you once lived. [8] But now you must rid yourselves of all such things as these: anger, rage, malice, slander, and filthy language from your lips. [9] Do not lie to each other, since you have taken off your old self with its practices [10] and have put on the new self, which is being renewed in knowledge in the image of its Creator. [11] Here there is no Greek or Jew, circumcised or uncircumcised, barbarian, Scythian, slave or free, but Christ is all, and is in all. [12] Therefore, as God's chosen people, holy and dearly loved, clothe yourselves with compassion, kindness, humility, gentleness and patience. [13] Bear with each other and forgive whatever grievances you may have against one another. Forgive as the Lord forgave you. [14] And over all these virtues put on love, which binds them all together in perfect unity. [15] Let the peace of Christ rule in your hearts, since as members of one body you were called to peace. And be thankful. [16] Let

Notes

the word of Christ dwell in you richly <u>as you teach and admonish</u> one another with all wisdom, and as you sing psalms, hymns and spiritual songs with gratitude in your hearts to God. [17] And whatever you do, whether in word or deed, do it all in the name of the Lord Jesus, giving thanks to God the Father through him."

b. A culture of learning is developed through an internal heart change, an acceptance that whole of life learning is what Christ instituted, the being and making of disciples.

Answering the challenges of our age

1. <u>Hebrews   5:11-6:11</u> (NIV) 6:4-6Ref— <u>Heb 10:26-31</u> [11] "We have much to say about this, but it is hard to explain because you are slow to learn. [12] In fact, though by this time you ought to be teachers, you need someone to teach you the elementary truths of God's word all over again. You need milk, not solid food! [13] Anyone who lives on milk, being still an infant, is not acquainted with the teaching about righteousness. [14] But solid food is for the mature, who by constant use have trained themselves to distinguish good from evil."

Notes

Notes

Part 2
RAISING NEW LEADERS

How To Use Part 2

How to *use each section of part two*

1. **Each session is meant to last one hour.**

   ₪ Each session is meant to be primarily interactive.

   ₪ At the start of each session is a section to be filled in by the student. The notes accompanying the session should preferably be read by the student at the end of the session in order to make the event as interactive as possible.

2. **Each session is broken down into four consistent parts.**

   Part one: *A key question (15 minutes)*

   ₪ Everyone is put into groups of 2-4 and asked to take 5 minutes to answer one key question.

   ₪ Feedback is then taken for a further ten minutes from each of the groups.

   Part two: *How would I answer that? (15 minutes)*

   ₪ Folk can get into groups again or sit on their own. They are required to consider a series of rapid questions over 7 minutes and they are encouraged to write down their answers.

   ₪ Feedback is then taken on an individual basis rather than as a group.

   Part three: *God's heart - personal prayer and reflection (15 minutes)*

   ₪ The group is encouraged to meditate on a series of probing questions

   Part four: *Things you need to consider (15 minutes)*

   ₪ A time for the course deliverer to recap key points which help underpin learning.

3. **The whole session is aimed at encouraging engagement with God's heart and God's word, His requirements and how they can achieve them.**

Session 1 Your Leadership Call Date:___

Romans 12:3 (KJV) "For I say, through the grace given unto me, to every man that is among you, not to think of himself more highly than he ought to think; but to think soberly, according as God hath dealt to every man the measure of faith.

Part one: *A key question (15 minutes)*

Part two: *How would I answer that? (15 minutes)*

Part three: *God's heart - personal prayer and reflection (15 minutes)*

Part four: *Things you need to consider (15 minutes)*

Your Leadership Call.

Part one: ***A key question (15 minutes)***

1. **List what you consider the bible states as essential traits in leadership?**

    Romans 12:3 (KJV) "For I say, through the grace given unto me, to every man that is among you, not to think of himself more highly than he ought to think; but to think soberly, according as God hath dealt to every man the measure of faith."

    a. Is a heart after God an essential trait in leadership?

        ₪ Love for God and people must be the main motivation. Why? Because real leadership is servant-hood.

        Deuteronomy 10:12 "And now, O Israel, what does the LORD your God ask of you but to fear the LORD your God, to walk in all his ways, to love him, to serve the LORD your God with all your heart and with all your soul. (C/f) Micah 6:8 He has showed you, O man, what is good. And what does the LORD require of you? To act justly and to love mercy and to walk humbly with your God."

    b. Is a teachable spirit an essential trait in leadership?

        i.   A dogmatic leader is dangerous. One who thinks he has a monopoly on the truth is in error.

        Psalms 143:10 "Teach me to do your will, for you are my God; may your good Spirit lead me on level ground."

    c. Is being full of the Holy Spirit an essential trait in leadership?

        Ephesians 5:18 "Do not get drunk on wine, which leads to debauchery. Instead, be filled with the Spirit."

    d. An ability to promote unity in the body would be considered by many to be a necessary trait in leadership.

₪   Someone who can handle disagreements in the body with sensitivity is an important contributor to church life.

> 2 Timothy 2:25 "Those who oppose him he must gently instruct, in the hope that God will grant them repentance leading them to a knowledge of the truth,"

e.   Is submissiveness an essential trait in leadership?

₪ Should those who ask others to submit have to be submissive? Hebrews 13:17 "Obey your leaders and submit to their authority. They keep watch over you as men who must give an account. Obey them so that their work will be a joy, not a burden, for that would be of no advantage to you.

2.   **Should a leader have to know what the vision of the church is if he is to lead a group?**

₪ Paul could give leadership because he was envisioned by God

> Acts 16:9 During the night Paul had a vision of a man of Macedonia standing and begging him, "Come over to Macedonia and help us."

a.   Will a leader fully support church events if he is not envisioned?

> Hebrews 10:25 "Let us not give up meeting together, as some are in the habit of doing, but let us encourage one another-and all the more as you see the Day approaching."

b.   Is the ability to communicate an essential trait in leadership?

> 2 Timothy 2:2 "And the things you have heard me say in the presence of many witnesses entrust to reliable men who will also be qualified to teach others."

Part two: How would I answer that? (15 minutes)

1.   **Are you commissioned to be a leader?**

a.   What does it mean to be commissioned?

   ת Consider Isaiah, Jesus, Abraham, David.

b. Do you believe in your heart that you are called by God to ministry?

c. What is the nature of leadership?

      i. The nature of the commission is revealed by Paul who states, "I have become the church's servant" – Col 1:25.

      ii. To serve the church is to live out your destiny.

d. What words are used to describe commissioned leadership in a secular context?

e. What words are used in the Christian environment to describe leadership?

Part three: *God's heart - personal prayer and reflection (15 minutes)*

1. Do you think you can lead a group?

a. Some people are better one to one. For most, the willingness to lead a group will depend upon what kind of group they are asked to lead.

b. What kind of group do you see yourself leading now or in the future?

c. There are several reasons why some find difficulties in leading a group. What things would hold you back?

      i. Some may have tried in the past and have been let down by other Christians.

      Acts 15:37-38 "Barnabas wanted to take John, also called Mark, with them, {38} but Paul did not think it wise to take him, because he had deserted them in Pamphylia and had not continued with them in the work."

      ii. Some would like to, but they feel incompetent.

2 Corinthians 11:5 "But I do not think I am in the least inferior to those "super-apostles."

.

    iii. Some are afraid of failure. They would rather do nothing and not fail, than attempt to do something and fail.

    iv. Some want their own ministry and are simply waiting for the best possible offer, position or opportunity to come along.

1 Corinthians 10:24 "Nobody should seek his own good, but the good of others."

    v. Some have not been asked.

2. **How could you address those issues that hold someone back from pursuing their call?**

    a. Family life has been used as a reason why individuals cannot get actively involved or give their time. What excuses have you heard offered as a reason for not being able to serve the call upon their lives?

      ₪ 1 Timothy 3:5 "If anyone does not know how to manage his own family, how can he take care of God's church?"

      ₪ Excuses centred around the family include pregnancy, baby, school, holidays, teenagers need my time, university (don't see much of them) etc.

Part four: **Things you need to consider. (15 minutes)**

1. **You need a right perspective about yourself.**

    a. When God fills us with the Holy Spirit, He equips every single one of us.

1 Corinthians 12:7-9 "Now to each one the manifestation of the Spirit is given for the common good. {8} To one there is given through the Spirit the message of wisdom, to another the message of knowledge by means of the same Spirit, {9} to another faith by the same Spirit, to another gifts of healing by that one Spirit,"

b. God's perspective of Gideon was different from Gideon's perspective of himself.

Judges 6:11-19 "The angel of the LORD came and sat down under the oak in Ophrah that belonged to Joash the Abiezrite, where his son Gideon was threshing wheat in a winepress to keep it from the Midianites. {12} When the angel of the LORD appeared to Gideon, he said, "The LORD is with you, mighty warrior." {13} "But sir," Gideon replied, "if the LORD is with us, why has all this happened to us? Where are all his wonders that our fathers told us about when they said, `Did not the LORD bring us up out of Egypt?' But now the LORD has abandoned us and put us into the hand of Midian." {14} The LORD turned to him and said, "Go in the strength you have and save Israel out of Midian's hand. Am I not sending you?" {15} "But Lord," Gideon asked, "how can I save Israel? My clan is the weakest in Manasseh, and I am the least in my family." {16} The LORD answered, "I will be with you, and you will strike down all the Midianites together." {17} Gideon replied, "If now I have found favour in your eyes, give me a sign that it is really you talking to me. {18} Please do not go away until I come back and bring my offering and set it before you." And the LORD said, "I will wait until you return." {19} Gideon went in, prepared a young goat, and from an ephah of flour he made bread without yeast. Putting the meat in a basket and its broth in a pot, he brought them out and offered them to him under the oak"

2. How do we build a good self image?

2 Corinthians 12:10 "That is why, for Christ's sake, I delight in weaknesses, in insults, in hardships, in persecutions, in difficulties. For when I am weak, then I am strong. " (C/f) Colossians 2:8 See to it that no one takes you captive through hollow and deceptive philosophy, which depends on human tradition and the basic principles of this world rather than on Christ."

a. Nevertheless God wants to build up our identity in Him. We are part of the most amazing family in the world.

John 1:12-13 "Yet to all who received him, to those who believed in his name, he gave the right to become children of God-- {13} children born not of natural descent, nor of human decision or a husband's will, but born of God."

b.   Certain truth is fundamental to a good self image

c.   Though within ourselves we are weak, through Him we have divine power.

2 Peter 1:3 "His divine power has given us everything we need for life and godliness through our knowledge of him who called us by his own glory and goodness." (C/f) 2 Corinthians 4:7 But we have this treasure in jars of clay to show that this all-surpassing power is from God and not from us."

d.   We have a competency that comes from Christ.

2 Corinthians 3:4-6 "Such confidence as this is ours through Christ before God. {5} Not that we are competent in ourselves to claim anything for ourselves, but our competence comes from God. {6} He has made us competent as ministers of a new covenant-not of the letter but of the Spirit; for the letter kills, but the Spirit gives life."

e.   Whatever we were, we have acquired a new status, that of royalty.

1 Peter 2:9 "But you are a chosen people, a royal priesthood, a holy nation, a people belonging to God, that you may declare the praises of him who called you out of darkness into his wonderful light."

f.   What will happen to me if I fail?

Jeremiah 17:7-10 "But blessed is the man who trusts in the LORD, whose confidence is in him. {8} He will be like a tree planted by the water that sends out its roots by the stream. It does not fear when heat comes; its leaves are always green. It has no worries in a year of drought and never fails to bear fruit." {9} The heart is deceitful above all things and beyond cure. Who can understand it? {10} "I the LORD search the heart and examine the mind, to reward a man according to his conduct, according to what his deeds deserve."

Session 2 Personal Development Date_____

Part one: ***A key question (15 minutes)***

Part two: ***How would I answer that? (15 minutes)***

Part three: *God's heart - personal prayer and reflection (15 minutes)*

Part four: *Things you need to consider (15 minutes)*

Personal Development

Colossians 1:24-29 "Now I rejoice in what was suffered for you, and I fill up in my flesh what is still lacking in regard to Christ's afflictions, for the sake of his body, which is the church. 25 I have become its servant by the commission God gave me to present to you the word of God in its fullness- 26 the mystery that has been kept hidden for ages and generations, but is now disclosed to the saints. 27 To them God has chosen to make known among the Gentiles the glorious riches of this mystery, which is Christ in you, the hope of glory. 28 We proclaim him, admonishing and teaching everyone with all wisdom, so that we may present everyone perfect in Christ. 29 To this end I labor, struggling with all his energy, which so powerfully works in me."

Part one: A key question (15 minutes)

1. **What happens when we have the unrestricted revelation that Christ lives in us?**

    a. This is described as a mystery hidden for generations but now revealed.

    b. This mystery enables us to present everyone perfect in Christ.

2. **Two elements are required to come together to achieve this in our own personal lives. First, we must learn to cope with suffering in the course of serving Christ, and secondly, we must grow in the word of God.**

    a. We will be aided in this course if we are willing to commit to becoming honest and open about our personal growth.

        i. School is a good analogy for life. If you want to keep growing you have to be willing to keep learning.

        ii. Can you identify in yourself what aspects of spiritual growth you are lacking?

        iii. If change is to happen and growth is to take place, then we must become willing to face our deficiencies without fear or anxiety.

b. Will you commit to serving despite hardship?

₪ Most people struggle with suffering in the course of serving Christ.

John 15:20 (NIV) — 20 "Remember what I told you: 'A servant is not greater than his master.' If they persecuted me, they will persecute you also. If they obeyed my teaching, they will obey yours also."

c. Commit to becoming absolutely reliant on God.

₪ Effective Christian leaders know the source of their srength and confidence. The first responsibility of every Christian leader is to abide in God's strength. It is a healthy exercise in self-awareness to understand the true source of your strength. What do you rely on to prop you up in a difficult time?

Part two: *How would I answer that? (15 minutes)*

1. **Personal growth demands a developing character.**

   a. But how do we asses growth?

   b. How is character shaped?

   ₪ Character is shaped in the company of others.

   c. Probing questions.

      i. How well do you get on with others?

      ii. Do you like yourself?

      iii. How do you cope with disappointment?

      iv. How do you cope with rejection?

      v. How do you cope with being challenged about your behaviour?

2. **The transformation of the individual into the likeness of Christ should be our desire.**

> *Luke 9:23–24 (NIV) — "Then he said to them all: "Whoever wants to be my disciple must deny themselves and take up their cross daily and follow me. 24 For whoever wants to save their life will lose it, but whoever loses their life for me will save it."*

> *2 Corinthians 3:18 (NIV) — "And we all, who with unveiled faces contemplate the Lord's glory, are being transformed into his image with ever-increasing glory, which comes from the Lord, who is the Spirit."*

Part three: **God's heart - personal prayer and reflection (15 minutes)**

1. **What part does the Bible play in your personal development?**

   a. Do you believe God speaks through the written word?

      i. Personal growth commences with the word, but do you read the word?

      > *Joshua 1:8–9 (NIV) — "Keep this Book of the Law always on your lips; meditate on it day and night, so that you may be careful to do everything written in it. Then you will be prosperous and successful. 9 Have I not commanded you? Be strong and courageous. Do not be afraid; do not be discouraged, for the LORD your God will be with you wherever you go."*

      ii. If the bible is not the foundation for your understanding of the world, what dangers does that present to your leadership?

      iii. Unless the word is your guide, it is impossible to resist people pressure.

2. **Do you believe that God speaks through the prophetic word?**

   a. Do you keep a journal of what God has said to you? Do you treasure it?

      > *2 Timothy 1:13–14 (NIV) — "What you heard from me, keep as the pattern of sound teaching, with faith and love in Christ Jesus. 14 Guard the good deposit that was entrusted to you—guard it with the help of the Holy Spirit who lives in us."*

      i. Are you able to be open with what God has said to you?

ii. Do you feel you are living with compromise, given what God has said to you?

3. **Personal growth demands dealing with anxiety.**

a. Anxiety comes because you can't see a way out of a problem.

b. Share the problem and the anxiety will decrease. Some things appear to be larger than they are.

c. Prayer reduces anxiety, cast your anxiety on Him. Cast your anxiety on Him for He cares for you.

d. Personal growth in the small things, enables us to face and deal with the larger issues that bring anxiety into our lives. The opposition can be overwhelming if we have never learned to overcome little challenges.

Nehemiah 4:1–5 (NIV) — "When Sanballat heard that we were rebuilding the wall, he became angry and was greatly incensed. He ridiculed the Jews, 2 and in the presence of his associates and the army of Samaria, he said, "What are those feeble Jews doing? Will they restore their wall? Will they offer sacrifices? Will they finish in a day? Can they bring the stones back to life from those heaps of rubble—burned as they are?" 3 Tobiah the Ammonite, who was at his side, said, "What they are building—even a fox climbing up on it would break down their wall of stones!" 4 Hear us, our God, for we are despised. Turn their insults back on their own heads. Give them over as plunder in a land of captivity. 5 Do not cover up their guilt or blot out their sins from your sight, for they have thrown insults in the face of the builders."

Part four: Things you need to consider (15 minutes)

1. **Are you willing to work through trying difficulties?**

2. **Christians are not exempt from trouble and pain in the world.**

3. **Are you willing to work through misunderstandings?**

4. **Your motives will be questioned and misunderstood by others.**

5. **You will face an ongoing burden for the church and your ministry.**

2 Corinthians 11:24–28 (NIV) — "Five times I received from the Jews the forty lashes minus one. 25 Three times I was beaten with rods, once I was pelted with stones, three times I was shipwrecked, I spent a night and a day in the open sea, 26 I have been constantly on the move. I have been in danger from rivers, in danger from bandits, in danger from my fellow Jews, in danger from Gentiles; in danger in the city, in danger in the country, in danger at sea; and in danger from false believers. 27 I have labored and toiled and have often gone without sleep; I have known hunger and thirst and have often gone without food; I have been cold and naked. 28 Besides everything else, I face daily the pressure of my concern for all the churches."

NOTES

Session 3 Loyalty to God, Family and the Community. Date_____

Part one: *A key question (15 minutes)*

Part two: *How would I answer that? (15 minutes)*

Part three: **God's heart - personal prayer and reflection (15 minutes)**

Part four: **Things you need to consider (15 minutes)**

Loyalty to God, Family and the Community

Part one: *A key question (15 minutes)*

1. **What motivates loyalty in heaven?**

Part two: *How would I answer that? (15 minutes)*

1. **How do I maintain loyalty towards myself?**

2. **How do I maintain loyalty towards God?**

    a. Those who failed;

        i.   Saul

        ii. Judas

        iii. Aaron

        iv. Peter

    b. I must love Him devotionally.

        ₪ The Psalmist speaks about the devotional lifestyle through which the word of God is constantly meditated upon.

    c. I must keep the call before me.

        ₪ Paul kept the call of God before him.

    d. Acknowledge the temptations that come your way.

        ₪ Ask for prayer when the distractions come, don't pretend you are not facing challenges.

   e. Keep yourself accountable.

   f. Choose company that does not draw you away from God.

> *Psalm 1:1–3 (NIV) — "Blessed is the one who does not walk in step with the wicked or stand in the way that sinners take or sit in the company of mockers, 2 but whose delight is in the law of the LORD, and who meditates on his law day and night. 3 That person is like a tree planted by streams of water, which yields its fruit in season and whose leaf does not wither— whatever they do prospers."*

3. How do I maintain loyalty in family relationships?

> *Matthew 5:27–30 (NIV) — "You have heard that it was said, 'You shall not commit adultery.' 28 But I tell you that anyone who looks at a woman lustfully has already committed adultery with her in his heart. 29 If your right eye causes you to stumble, gouge it out and throw it away. It is better for you to lose one part of your body than for your whole body to be thrown into hell. 30 And if your right hand causes you to stumble, cut it off and throw it away. It is better for you to lose one part of your body than for your whole body to go into hell."*

₪ If you want to remain loyal to God, your spouse, your friends, and your community, then you need to choose your company carefully; prioritise spending time with people who help you grow in your faith.

   a. Don't share secrets with an inappropriate person.

   b. Treat family members with respect.

> *1 Timothy 5:1–2 (NIV) — "Do not rebuke an older man harshly, but exhort him as if he were your father. Treat younger men as brothers, 2 older women as mothers, and younger women as sisters, with absolute purity."*

Part three: *God's heart - personal prayer and reflection (15 minutes)*

1. Loyalty to the community requires what commitments?

   a. To be faithful to the community you must be around to serve it.

     i. How can I create time to serve in the community.

     ii. What forms of service can I consistently give?

b. To be faithful to the community you must be willing to feed the sheep.

Luke 16:10-13 "Whoever can be trusted with very little can also be trusted with much, and whoever is dishonest with very little will also be dishonest with much. 11 So if you have not been trustworthy in handling worldly wealth, who will trust you with true riches? 12 And if you have not been trustworthy with someone else's property, who will give you property of your own? 13 "No servant can serve two masters. Either he will hate the one and love the other, or he will be devoted to the one and despise the other. You cannot serve both God and Money."

c. To be faithful to the community you must be faithful to God

Part four: Things you need to consider (15 minutes)

1. How to know if you are straying.

a. When the word of God is no longer playing a pivotal part in your life you are straying.

b. We are commissioned to apply the word of God; God's word must never become subservient to philosophies or ideologies of the age.

    ₪ "The word of God must not be sacrificed on the altar of public opinion"

c. When "ego" becomes dominant, we are straying.

     i. When you begin to feel rejection and hurt over little things and become easily overwhelmed with issues.

     ii. When time with God only happens in meetings that you are leading, speaking at, or have to attend.

     iii. When prayer is absent from your personal devotions and in truth, they don't exist except in the company of others.

iv. When you find it easy to state a white lie-and it doesn't trouble you greatly, then you are straying.

v. When you know you are pleasing people, rather than God.

1 John 2:15–17 (NIV) — 15 Do not love the world or anything in the world. If anyone loves the world, love for the Father is not in them. 16 For everything in the world—the lust of the flesh, the lust of the eyes, and the pride of life—comes not from the Father but from the world. 17 The world and its desires pass away, but whoever does the will of God lives forever.

NOTES

Session 4 Doing Discipleship Well. Date_____

Part one: *A key question (15 minutes)*

Part two: *How would I answer that? (15 minutes)*

Part three: *God's heart - personal prayer and reflection (15 minutes)*

Part four: *Things you need to consider (15 minutes)*

Part three: *God's heart - personal prayer and reflection (15 minutes)*

Doing Discipleship Well

Part one: *A key question (15 minutes)*

1. **How can we achieve honest relationships?**

    a. Examples exist;

        i.   David and Jonathan

        ii. Barnabas and Paul

2. **First, commit to love everyone on your team, do honest relationships.**

    1 Peter 1:22 "Now that you have purified yourselves by obeying the truth so that you have sincere love for your brothers, love one another deeply, from the heart."

Part two: *How would I answer that? (15 minutes)*

1. **What kind of people should we invest our time in as a priority?**

    ₪ Leader's time is often limited, and free time is usually non-existent or under pressure.

    ₪ Yet if leaders want to reproduce themselves and leave behind competent ministries, then they will have to disciple others.

    ₪ If a leader does consider the investment of time to train others a worthwhile endeavour, then it will be reflected in that, no matter how busy he is, he will create the time to do it.

    ₪ Whilst leaders should give pastoral time to any needy members, leaders always need to chose to invest time to train people they consider to have some of the following qualities.

a. Leaders look for people who are:

    i. Faithful.

    1 Samuel 2:22-26 "Now Eli, who was very old, heard about everything his sons were doing to all Israel and how they slept with the women who served at the entrance to the Tent of Meeting. {23} So he said to them, "Why do you do such things? I hear from all the people about these wicked deeds of yours. {24} No, my sons; it is not a good report that I hear spreading among the LORD's people. {25} If a man sins against another man, God may mediate for him; but if a man sins against the LORD, who will intercede for him?" His sons, however, did not listen to their father's rebuke, for it was the LORD's will to put them to death. {26} And the boy Samuel continued to grow in stature and in favour with the LORD and with men."

    ii. Leaders look for people with a consistent lifestyle.

    iii. Leaders look for people who are filled with the Spirit.

    iv. Leaders look for people who are teachable and humble.

    v. Leaders look for people who are intimate with God.

    vi. Leaders look for people who are readers of the word.

    vii. Leaders look for people who are prayerful.

₪ It is important that we try and understand the people we are trying to disciple.

2. Why do people attend church?

₪ There are different reasons why people attend church. If you want to build strong disciples you first need to discern those who are purely attending out of religious duty, or those who really want to go on with God.

₪ There are those who are with you for the long term and those who were simply developing for the next stage of their journey with the Lord.

₪ It seems counter-intuitive, but you must invest as a priority in those who are going to carry forward the long-term strategy God has released for the church.

Part three: God's heart - personal prayer and reflection (15 minutes)

1. **How do you build and amazing team?**

    a. Building loyal disciples.

        i. Help them face their distractions.

        ₪ If you're going to build true disciples of Jesus Christ then you need to spot the distractions in their lives and help them deal with them.

        ₪ It is important not to be frustrated with those who are coasting in their spirituality, but rather love them and help them make good decisions towards growth.

    b. Build a bible believing team.

        John 6:53–57 (NIV) — "Jesus said to them, "Very truly I tell you, unless you eat the flesh of the Son of Man and drink his blood, you have no life in you. 54 Whoever eats my flesh and drinks my blood has eternal life, and I will raise them up at the last day. 55 For my flesh is real food and my blood is real drink. 56 Whoever eats my flesh and drinks my blood remains in me, and I in them. 57 Just as the living Father sent me and I live because of the Father, so the one who feeds on me will live because of "

    c. Build faith into the team.

        i. Cultivate their sense of call.

        ii. Cultivate an environment where people share testimony.

        iii. Invest in those who are teachable.

        iv. Invest in those who are mature, as they will have probably dealt with their ego and behave in more appropriate ways.

        v. Invest in those who take every opportunity to promote and serve God's plan.

Numbers 14:5–9 (NIV) — "Then Moses and Aaron fell facedown in front of the whole Israelite assembly gathered there. 6 Joshua son of Nun and Caleb son of Jephunneh, who were among those who had explored the land, tore their clothes 7 and said to the entire Israelite assembly, "The land we passed through and explored is exceedingly good. 8 If the LORD is pleased with us, he will lead us into that land, a land flowing with milk and honey, and will give it to us. 9 Only do not rebel against the LORD. And do not be afraid of the people of the land, because we will devour them. Their protection is gone, but the LORD is with us. Do not be afraid of them."

    d.   Invest in people who are willing to share their lives and help the team succeed.

    e.   Build a team committed to small groups.

        i.   A group is the backbone of church.

        ii.   Every leader is a pastoral worker.

        iii.   You are there to provide pastoral care for the sheep.

2.   There is only so much that an eldership can do. Group leaders provide extended pastoral support.

Ezekiel 34:5 "So they were scattered because there was no shepherd, and when they were scattered they became food for all the wild animals."

    a.   They know the condition of every sheep in the group.

Proverbs 27:23 "Be sure you know the condition of your flocks, give careful attention to your herds"

    b.   The sheep will rightly begin to lean on the leaders and require help and support.

John 21:17 "The third time he said to him, "Simon son of John, do you love me?" Peter was hurt because Jesus asked him the third time, "Do you love me?" He said, "Lord, you know all things; you know that I love you. " Jesus said, "Feed my sheep."

    c.   The cost is great. If you are called of God then learning how to care for groups is part of God's plan for your life.

Part four: *Things you need to consider (15 minutes)*

1. Teach disciples how to handle difficult discussions

a. Tackle issues before they spiral out of control.

   ₪ Very often misunderstandings spiral out of control, and if left to become compounded, are impossible to fix in time.

b. Advise them that God honours righteousness.

   Psalm 37:34–37 (NIV) — " Hope in the LORD and keep his way. He will exalt you to inherit the land; when the wicked are destroyed, you will see it. 35 I have seen a wicked and ruthless man flourishing like a luxuriant native tree, 36 but he soon passed away and was no more; though I looked for him, he could not be found. 37 Consider the blameless, observe the upright; a future awaits those who seek peace."

c. If chairing a conflict.

   i. Treat everyone fairly and gently.

   Proverbs 15:1 (NIV) — "A gentle answer turns away wrath, but a harsh word stirs up anger."

   ii. Encourage the disciple not to see conflict as a failure, but rather as an opportunity to demonstrate the love that the gospel holds out to humanity.

   iii. Encourage a listening ear.

   iv. Be aware that there might be a root issue which bears no resemblance to the presenting problem

   v. Don't allow your sense of moral outrage to disqualify you from being an honest broker.

   vi. Deal with the issue presented, don't allow other issues to cloud the one you are seeking to bring peace into.

NOTES

Session 5 The Vision. Date_____

Part one: *A key question (15 minutes)*

Part two: *How would I answer that? (15 minutes)*

Part three: *God's heart - personal prayer and reflection (15 minutes)*

Part four: *Things you need to consider (15 minutes)*

Part three: *God's heart - personal prayer and reflection (15 minutes)*

The Vision

Part one: *A key question (15 minutes)*

1. **What is the big picture you see for our church?**

    a. Effective Christian leaders see the big picture.

    b. You need to have a clear vision to effectively communicate it.

    > Jeremiah 1:11-12 *"The word of the LORD came to me "What do you see, Jeremiah?" "I see the branch of an almond tree," I replied. {12} The LORD said to me, "You have seen correctly, for I am watching to see that my word is fulfilled."*

Part two: *How would I answer that? (15 minutes)*

1. **What is the vision?**

2. **Have we as a church got the right vision?**

Part three: *God's heart - personal prayer and reflection (15 minutes)*

1. **What happens if we do not communicate the vision?**

    a. People find their own.

    > Jeremiah 8:6 *"I have listened attentively, but they do not say what is right. No one repents of his wickedness, saying, "What have I done?" Each pursues his own course like a horse charging into battle."*

Part four: *Things you need to consider (15 minutes)*

1. **How does a leader get a hold of the vision?**

    a. Abraham's vision gives pointers to where the vision should come from.

Genesis 13:12-17 "Abram lived in the land of Canaan, while Lot lived among the cities of the plain and pitched his tents near Sodom. {13} Now the men of Sodom were wicked and were sinning greatly against the LORD. {14} The LORD said to Abram after Lot had parted from him, "Lift up your eyes from where you are and look north and south, east and west. {15} All the land that you see I will give to you and your offspring forever. {16} I will make your offspring like the dust of the earth, so that if anyone could count the dust, then your offspring could be counted. {17} Go, walk through the length and breadth of the land, for I am giving it to you."

      i.   Lot chose to go his own way, but Abraham waited upon God's direction.

b.   Effective Christian leaders are those who look beyond attendance figures. They look beyond today. They want to develop people, not just produce events. Having the big picture changes the way we approach ministry.

c.   Benefits of having the big picture:

      i.   We will be less concerned with programs, more concerned with people.

      ii.   We will have more patience with those who are different from us.

      iii.   We will focus more on ministry and less on programming.

      iv.   We will be less concerned with our rights and more concerned with our responsibilities.

2. How do we help everyone on the team catch the vision?

a.   Don't assume everyone knows the vision.

b.   Don't assume they have subscribed to the vision. It is essential that you take your core leadership team through the vision of the church, line by line.

c.   Praise those who have been faithful to the vision.

1 Samuel 17:34–37 (NIV) — "But David said to Saul, "Your servant has been keeping his father's sheep. When a lion or a bear came and carried off a sheep from the flock, 35 I went after it, struck it and rescued the sheep from its mouth. When it turned on me, I seized it by its hair, struck it and killed it. 36 Your servant has killed both the lion and the bear; this uncircumcised Philistine will be like one of them, because he has defied the armies of the living God. 37 The LORD who rescued me from the paw of the lion and the paw of the bear will rescue me from the hand of this Philistine." Saul said to David, "Go, and the LORD be with you."

d.   Encourage people to talk about the vision.

e.   Encourage them to pray for revelation into the vision and not just knowledge of it.

2 Kings 6:17 (NIV) — "And Elisha prayed, "Open his eyes, LORD, so that he may see." Then the LORD opened the servant's eyes, and he looked and saw the hills full of horses and chariots of fire all around Elisha."

Joshua 6:2 (NIV) — "Then the LORD said to Joshua, "See, I have delivered Jericho into your hands, along with its king and its fighting men."

f.   Map out team aims.

   i.   Groups with a specific focus can offer the best means of reaching those kinds of people. e.g. youth, senior citizens or single parents.

   ii.   Focusing on people groups means becoming familiar with the needs, difficulties and opportunities, to serve that particular group.

   iii. The integration of people groups into church life will present the biggest challenge to this generation. The reason is simple; society continues to fragment in many ways; reaching fragmented people groups then will become a vital area of focus for the church.

   iv.   People's lives are so busy, specialised, dedicated and focused that groups could provide a meeting point for the fragmented communities we find ourselves living in.

g.   Mapping out the group vision.

   i.   Explaining how the vision fits into the vision of the church, helps group cohesion and purpose.

   ₪ Whatever kind of group we develop, pastoral care is an important part of the group function. While a leader of the group is essential, old methods of pastoring are not. Where in the past, one man was expected to pastor a group; now, we need to learn new approaches of caring for each other. Every member of the group should take part in caring for the others.

ii. Most people can only relate to a finite number of people at one time. Discipleship groups provide a framework for both relationships and expression of ministry. Relationships can only develop by relating. The discipleship group is one of the main ways to develop close, meaningful relationships with others in the body.

h. Teach the group vision.

Ephesians 4:14 "Then we will no longer be infants, tossed back and forth by the waves, and blown here and there by every wind of teaching and by the cunning and craftiness of men in their deceitful scheming."

i. Pray the vision into the group.

Psalms 32:6 "Therefore let everyone who is godly pray to you while you may be found; surely when the mighty waters rise, they will not reach him."

ii. Map out how the team is going to win souls and develop people within the vision.

Colossians 1:5-6 "the faith and love that spring from the hope that is stored up for you in heaven and that you have already heard about in the word of truth, the gospel {6} that has come to you. All over the world this gospel is bearing fruit and growing, just as it has been doing among you since the day you heard it and understood God's grace in all its truth."

iii. Celebrate all the victories that God gives the group.

₪ Worship becomes more intense when people feel that their lives are fulfilling the purposes of God. In a smaller group there is greater opportunity to be involved in more personal and intimate worship of our wonderful Lord, especially where the group members feel their lives are productive.

Psalms 100:2 "Worship the LORD with gladness; come before him with joyful songs."

Session 6 Difficult Issues Facing Leaders. Date_____

Part one: *A key question (15 minutes)*

Part two: *How would I answer that? (15 minutes)*

Part three: *God's heart - personal prayer and reflection (15 minutes)*

Part four: *Things you need to consider (15 minutes)*

Difficult Issues Facing Leaders

Part one: ***A key question (15 minutes)***

1. What tensions and difficulties can growth and blessing bring?

a. When God allows growth, it brings with it the possibility of the kind of tensions that result in tearing and division, instead of the growth that produces a healthy birthing of a new work, ministry or church. Tearing and division are the result of unresolved problems. Sometimes these problems are hidden and wilful, at other times they are the result of simple misunderstandings.

b. Leaders who relate to individuals in ministry, need to embrace the principle of release.

   i. Jacob's father in law, Laban, had difficulty in allowing Jacob to go.

   Genesis 30:25-27 "After Rachel gave birth to Joseph, Jacob said to Laban, "Send me on my way so I can go back to my own homeland. {26} Give me my wives and children, for whom I have served you, and I will be on my way. You know how much work I've done for you." {27} But Laban said to him, "If I have found favour in your eyes, please stay. I have learned by divination that the LORD has blessed me because of you."

   ii. Although Laban wanted Jacob to prosper, there was a bit of self about his attitude.

   Genesis 30:28 He added, "Name your wages, and I will pay them."

   iii. This attitude was shared by other members of his household.

   Genesis 31:1 "Jacob heard that Laban's sons were saying, "Jacob has taken everything our father owned and has gained all this wealth from what belonged to our father."

c. Because ministry needs to find expression, tensions will emerge if an individual is not released.

   ₪ Jacob began to feel claustrophobic, and when God told him to leave, he chose to do it in secret rather than in an open way.

> *Genesis 31:3 "Then the LORD said to Jacob, "Go back to the land of your fathers and to your relatives, and I will be with you." (C/f) Genesis 31:20 Moreover, Jacob deceived Laban the Aramean by not telling him he was running away."*

d.   Cultivating success is a gift we must acquire.

   i.   Leaders sometimes find ungodly attitudes of jealousy, envy, fear and insecurity surfacing when others around them begin to flow in blessing and growth.

> *Psalms 68:16 "Why gaze in envy, O rugged mountains, at the mountain where God chooses to reign, where the LORD himself will dwell forever?"*

₪ Saul is an example of a leader whose envy and jealousy defined his relationship with David. Everything David did could only be seen through jealous eyes.

> *1 Samuel 18:9 "And from that time on Saul kept a jealous eye on David."*

Part two: How would I answer that? (15 minutes)

1.   **How do we help people handle disagreements?**

   a.   Do godly people disagree?

   i.   When Paul and Barnabas had disagreements, the way they handled it is a model of how to handle disagreements that arise. Both men were pillars in the early church with huge reputations. Paul's letters became the cannon of Scripture and both of them were responsible for discipling many believers. In fact Barnabas had a hand in Paul's acceptance by the wider church community.

   > *Acts 9:27 "But Barnabas took him and brought him to the apostles. He told them how Saul on his journey had seen the Lord and that the Lord had spoken to him, and how in Damascus he had preached fearlessly in the name of Jesus."*

   ₪ The first dispute they had was with the believers from Judea teaching circumcision. They therefore decided to send a team to Jerusalem to clear up the dispute lest it spiral into a division between the Jews and the Gentiles. Acts 15:1-12

   ₪ Paul and Barnabas showed humility by going to Jerusalem to make themselves accountable. In doing so they did not display any kind of independent attitude.

b. Misunderstandings about personal vision can become a source of division, if not worked though.

i. If personal vision is not to become a source of division then the leaders and the visionary need to get together to agree how the vision fits into the corporate vision.

Amos 3:3 "Do two walk together unless they have agreed to do so?"

ii. God Himself is willing to be involved and use our unity as a conduit through which to bring our prayers to pass.

Matthew 18:19 "Again, I tell you that if two of you on earth agree about anything you ask for, it will be done for you by my Father in heaven."

2. Working with other leaders

₪ At some stage, leaders of all persuasions will be challenged with calls for church unity in the city and asked to fellowship with leaders from other churches.

₪ A leader will find such meetings less stressful if he is absolutely clear about his vision and boundaries. When a leader is clear about what is in his heart, he will feel secure to reach out to others.

a. Boundaries that will limit a leader include:

₪ The limits of his gifting.

₪ The boundaries of his gifting.

₪ Limited workers.

₪ Clashing and contrasting visions.

Part three: *God's heart - personal prayer and reflection (15 minutes)*

1. The Absalom Spirit

a. Absalom developed the spirit of the usurper and wanted to get rid of his father David.

b.   Why did he develop such a spirit?

c.   David did not deal with injustice and sin. When leaders do this it creates a sense of injustice and anger. Some people get it off their chests and express it, others keep it in and it becomes a source of deep frustration which later comes out in sinful ways.

d.   David did not show leadership, by failing to tackle Amnon's violation of Absalom's sister. He left a vacuum and deep sense of injustice.

> *2 Samuel 15:1-6 "In the course of time, Absalom provided himself with a chariot and horses and with fifty men to run ahead of him. {2} He would get up early and stand by the side of the road leading to the city gate. Whenever anyone came with a complaint to be placed before the king for a decision, Absalom would call out to him, "What town are you from?" He would answer, "Your servant is from one of the tribes of Israel." {3} Then Absalom would say to him, "Look, your claims are valid and proper, but there is no representative of the king to hear you." {4} And Absalom would add, "If only I were appointed judge in the land! Then everyone who has a complaint or case could come to me and I would see that he gets justice." {5} Also, whenever anyone approached him to bow down before him, Absalom would reach out his hand, take hold of him and kiss him. {6} Absalom behaved in this way toward all the Israelites who came to the king asking for justice, and so he stole the hearts of the men of Israel."*

e.   The spirit of the usurper is political in nature making promises.

> *2 Samuel 15:10-17 "Then Absalom sent secret messengers throughout the tribes of Israel to say, "As soon as you hear the sound of the trumpets, then say, `Absalom is king in Hebron.'" {11} Two hundred men from Jerusalem had accompanied Absalom. They had been invited as guests and went quite innocently, knowing nothing about the matter. {12} While Absalom was offering sacrifices, he also sent for Ahithophel the Gilonite, David's counsellor, to come from Giloh, his hometown. And so the conspiracy gained strength, and Absalom's following kept on increasing. {13} A messenger came and told David, "The hearts of the men of Israel are with Absalom." {14} Then David said to all his officials who were with him in Jerusalem, "Come! We must flee, or none of us will escape from Absalom. We must leave immediately, or he will move quickly to overtake us and bring ruin upon us and put the city to the sword." {15} The king's officials answered him, "Your servants are ready to do whatever our lord the king chooses." {16} The king set out, with his entire household following him; but he left ten concubines to take care*

of the palace. {17} So the king set out, with all the people following him, and they halted at a place some distance away."

f.   The spirit of the usurper works in secret before it becomes open.

Part four: *Things you need to consider (15 minutes)*

1.   **How do I pick people up when it all goes wrong?**

a.   The process of restoration.

b.   When a leader falls, what is the fallout?

₪   The effects can be devastating, leaving a broken family, devastated children, a scattered church and a discredited ministry. Yet, this is not when things should fall apart. Genuine love constrains believers to act in a Christ centred way, rather than leave when things go wrong. It is at this point that believers should come together to apply Christian love in a practical way. Restoration of fallen people should be our goal.

c.   Can a fallen leader be restored?

i.   To be restored, the fallen leader or ministry gift, faces "the moment of decision".

₪   When David faced Nathan the prophet, he faced his moment of decision.

ii.   The story begins with David's lust. In his selfishness, he had taken Bathsheba, another man's wife.

2 Samuel 11:2-5 "One evening David got up from his bed and walked around on the roof of the palace. From the roof he saw a woman bathing. The woman was very beautiful, {3} and David sent someone to find out about her. The man said, "Isn't this Bathsheba, the daughter of Eliam and the wife of Uriah the Hittite?" {4} Then David sent messengers to get her. She came to him, and he slept with her. (She had purified herself from her uncleanness.) Then she went back home. {5} The woman conceived and sent word to David, saying, "I am pregnant."

iii. When God chose to challenge him about his sin. He did so by telling a story of injustice perpetrated against a defenceless poor man.

2 Samuel 12:1-6 "The LORD sent Nathan to David. When he came to him, he said, "There were two men in a certain town, one rich and the other poor. {2} The rich man had a very large number of sheep and cattle, {3} but the poor man had nothing except one little ewe lamb he had bought. He raised it, and it grew up with him and his children. It shared his food, drank from his cup and even slept in his arms. It was like a daughter to him. {4} "Now a traveller came to the rich man, but the rich man refrained from taking one of his own sheep or cattle to prepare a meal for the traveller who had come to him. Instead, he took the ewe lamb that belonged to the poor man and prepared it for the one who had come to him."

iv. It was in this context that David faced the moment of truth.

2 Samuel 12:8 "I gave your master's house to you, and your master's wives into your arms. I gave you the house of Israel and Judah. And if all this had been too little, I would have given you even more."

v. His response to the moment of truth, determined God's response from that point forward. He repented, and so God forgave him, but not without a personal cost. 2 Samuel 12:11-17

d. Are there boundaries to the hope we offer a fallen leader?

i. The biblical language of restoration gives hope to the leaders or ministry gifts, that fall into sin.

ii. God calls the fallen to reason with Him about both their sin and state.

Isaiah 1:18 "Come now, let us reason together," says the LORD. "Though your sins are like scarlet, they shall be as white as snow; though they are red as crimson, they shall be like wool. (C/f) Isaiah 43:24-26 You have not bought any fragrant calamus for me, or lavished on me the fat of your sacrifices. But you have burdened me with your sins and wearied me with your offences. {25} "I, even I, am he who blots out your transgressions, for my own sake, and remembers your sins no more. {26} Review the past for me, let us argue the matter together; state the case for your innocence. (C/f) Micah 7:18-19 Who is a God like you, who pardons sin and forgives the transgression of the remnant of his inheritance? You do not stay angry forever but delight to show mercy. {19} You will again have compassion on us; you will tread our sins underfoot and hurl all our iniquities into the depths of the sea."

iii. If a leader has fallen into gross sin and has not admitted it, his fellow leaders should confront him.

James 5:19-20 "My brothers, if one of you should wander from the truth and someone should bring him back, {20} remember this: Whoever turns a sinner from the error of his way will save him from death and cover over a multitude of sins. (C/f) Matthew 18:12-15 "What do you think? If a man owns a hundred sheep, and one of them wanders away, will he not leave the ninety-nine on the hills and go to look for the one that wandered off? {13} And if he finds it, I tell you the truth, he is happier about that one sheep than about the ninety-nine that did not wander off. {14} In the same way your Father in heaven is not willing that any of these little ones should be lost. {15} "If your brother sins against you, go and show him his fault, just between the two of you. If he listens to you, you have won your brother over. (C/f) Jude {22-23} Be merciful to those who doubt; {23} snatch others from the fire and save them; to others show mercy, mixed with fear-hating even the clothing stained by corrupted flesh."

iv. We should be careful in the process, not to end up doing the same things that we are trying to save them from.

1 Corinthians 10:12 "So, if you think you are standing firm, be careful that you don't fall! (C/f) James 3:2 We all stumble in many ways. If anyone is never at fault in what he says, he is a perfect man, able to keep his whole body in check."

NOTES

Printed in Great Britain
by Amazon